BRONZE, BRASS, AND THE MYSTERIOUS ART OF BRAZING

Bronze, Brass and the Mysterious Art of Brazing: A Manual for Jewelers and Metal Sculptors

Kelsey Bogart

Cover design, photos, and text layout:
KJB Sculpture, kjbsculpture.com
Production@OneWorldPress.com
ISBN: 979-8-9861825-0-6
Ebook ISBN: 979-8-9861825-1-3

This book was printed in the United States of America by: ingramspark.com

ONE WORLD PRESS
890 Staley Lane
Chino Valley, AZ 86323
800-250-8178
production@oneworldpress.com

DEDICATION

For my Family, the Durhams
For my Spiritual Teacher, Lee Lozowick
For my Sangha, The Hohm Community

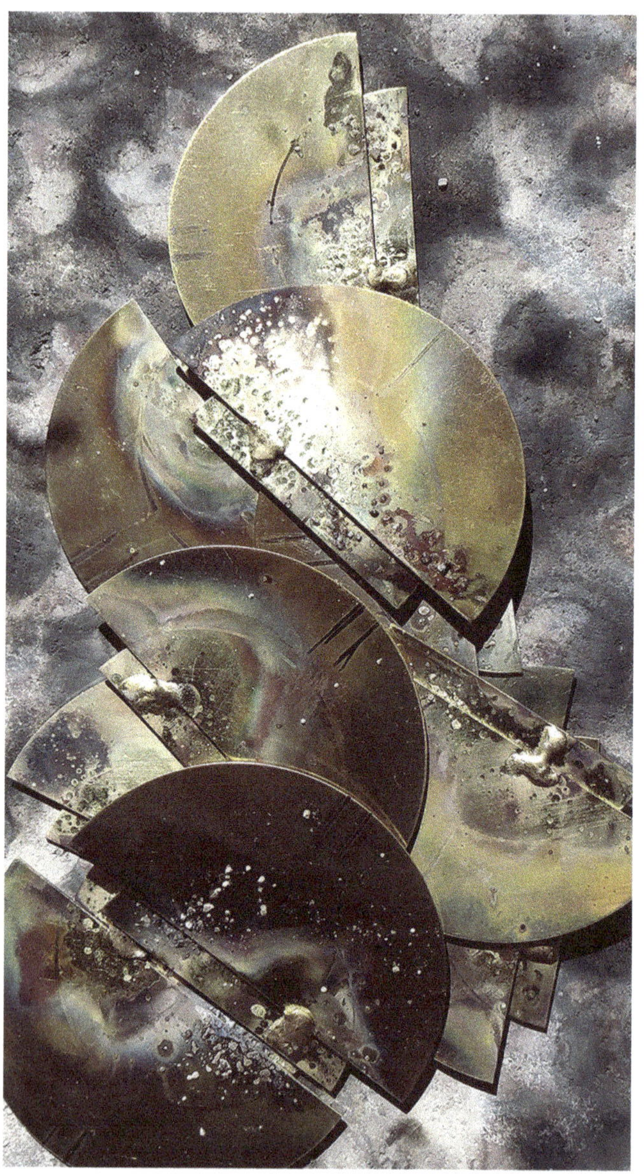

CONTENTS

ACKNOWLEDGMENTS

Carl Sweets MFA, Mentor par Excellence
Becky Fulker, Patient Adobe InDesign Coach
Mother Earth, for all her Gifts
Time, the Big Blabbermouth

INTRODUCTION

If you have advanced thus far into the first pages of this book, you are obviously interested in torch (or flame) brazing–defined as a form of non-fusion welding. The techniques that follow apply to my use of them with non-ferrous metals. I admire steel sculpture and jewelry, yet we all have self-imposed limitations. Torch brazing, however, may be applied to steel if you so choose.

My decision has been to *not* work with steel and concentrate on my love affair with copper and brass. Herein I will show you how I achieve certain effects–which are a bit like painting with fire (brush) and bronze (pigment) on brass and copper. If you have availed yourself of jewelry making classes, you may have noticed that many do not offer instruction in this technique. In my experience I have found oxygen and acetylene to be the best source of heat to create the necessary temperatures and most jewelry departments do not need this equipment. Sculpting departments do.

I also use torch brazing techniques to attach metal-to-metal instead of soldering. This requires that the forms be preheated to "tinning temperature". So, I believe that this could turn out to be a wonderful adventure for both of us and my fervent wish is that you will take what you learn in this manual and make it your own.

TOOLS AND EQUIPMENT

Oxygen (55 CF) and Acetylene (35 CF) welding tanks are nice medium sized ones and less expensive to fill. Smaller sizes work fine - Fully open the oxygen valve when brazing; open acetylene valve 1/4 turn. Important: do not allow pressure in acetylene secondary gauge enter the "red zone". Image 3.2.

Oxygen and Acetylene Dual Stage Gauges - Smith and Victor brands have great reputations. Purchase or rent your tanks first to determine what fittings (if any) you will require to attach your regulators to the tanks you have chosen. Image 3.2.

Goggles - Several styles are available at welding supply stores: #5 lens rating.

Smith Little Torch, lines, and tips - It is most efficient to purchase these items in a kit from a reputable dealer. I primarily use tip #4 in the work that I will be illustrating in this manual.

Ceramic soldering pads - I purchased high heat ones from Rio Grande Jewelry in a couple of sizes.

Striker - Or other torch lighting tool.

Pliers - Those already in your toolbox will probably suffice.

Medium-Duty Cutting Pliers - I purchased a nice pair from Ace Hardware under their brand.

Aviation Snips - I prefer Wiss brand straight cutters and even though they leave "nibble" marks, they are easy to use and versatile. You will develop hand and lower arm strength as you proceed with these snips, but I recommend doing so slowly to avoid strain. Image 5.1.

Dremel-Style Rotary Tool - For cutting bronze rods - with an 1/8" shank mandrel reinforced cutoff wheel attached. Referred to as a cut-off tool in text.

Sander that accommodates a 30 X 1 inch sanding belt - My preference. Other styles will work.

Hot Pot - Crock Pots work well.

Other finishing equipment of your choice -
For production work, I use a pneumatic angle grinder with 3M-style finishing pads and a vibrating tumbler with ceramic media, polishing liquid (purchased from Rio Grande Jewelry Supply), and water.
A Foredom-style flex shaft is helpful. These tools are pricey, so experimentation with cleaning techniques through workshops or metal sculpting classes is recommended. That way one may determine if there is artistic resonance before investing in specific equipment. Also, reference Chapter 6.

Vise - Larger, heavy-duty size preferred.

Tube Cutter - Small (not mini) copper tubing-style cutter—often used by plumbers.

Ruler/Tape Measure - Your preference.

Steel Plate - Look for a small piece, at least one foot square and ¼ inch thick. This item can often be found at a scrap yard, but is not compulsory. I find it useful in certain applications. Image 5.3 (steel plate with holes) and QR on manual cover.

Face Shield - Plastic and optional.

MATERIALS AND SUPPLIES

Bronze brazing rods - I prefer Harris low-fuming brand; various sizes, up to ¼ inch in diameter. Small samples: Image 2.1.

Clean sheet copper and brass - 22 gauge works well for brass. I use many gauges of copper.

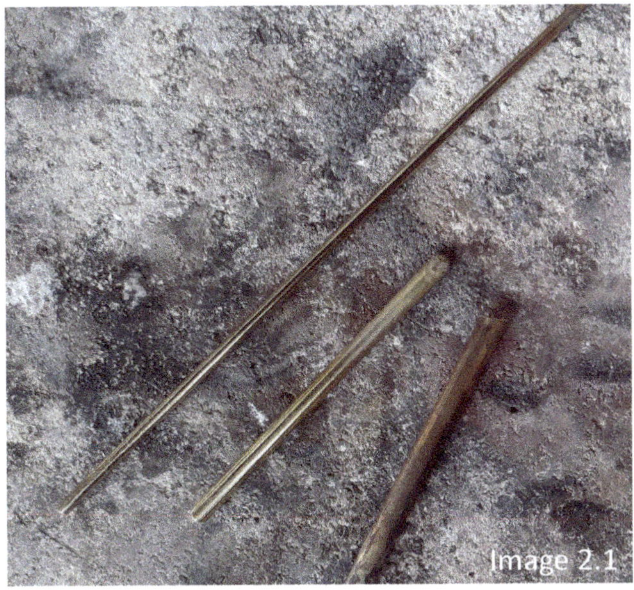

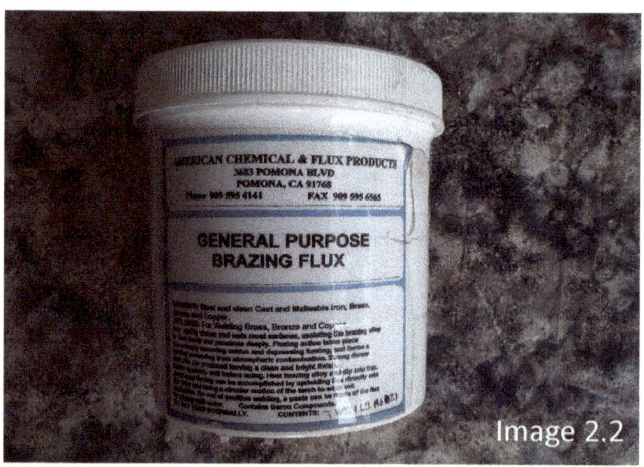

Image 2.2

Flux - I prefer a general purpose brazing flux manufactured by American Chemical or Harris. A white powder, the flux is used to absorb oxides created during the brazing process so as not to contaminate the join. Image 2.2.

Nitrile gloves - Tight fitting.

Dust Masks - Hardware store variety.

Thin leather gloves - Driving gloves work well.

Apron - Denim, canvas, or leather.

Sanding belts - To fit your sander. Fine—several of these in various grit grades and a couple of medium grit belts.

Dremel reinforced cutoff wheels - Typically found at Ace, Home Depot, or Lowe's, mounted on 1/8 inch shank mandrel.

White Vinegar - Purchased at grocery stores.

Sparex - "Pickle" from Rio Grande Jewelry Supply.

Baking Soda - For neutralizing acid solutions.

First Aid Kit - Bandaids, mostly. Eye cup or eye drops.

Bring Your Patience - Every smidgen.

CHAPTER 3

STUDIO SET-UP

I feel that the most important aspect of studio set-up is to have adequate ventilation. What this means is that it is essential to provide an exhaust system that adequately pulls air away from your person and studio during the brazing process, remaining mindful that fumes are not being vented toward anyone else. There are numerous harmful substances that occur in the torch brazing process; take good care of your lungs by not breathing them.

I use a high powered fan in an open window next to my brazing table. Image 3.1.

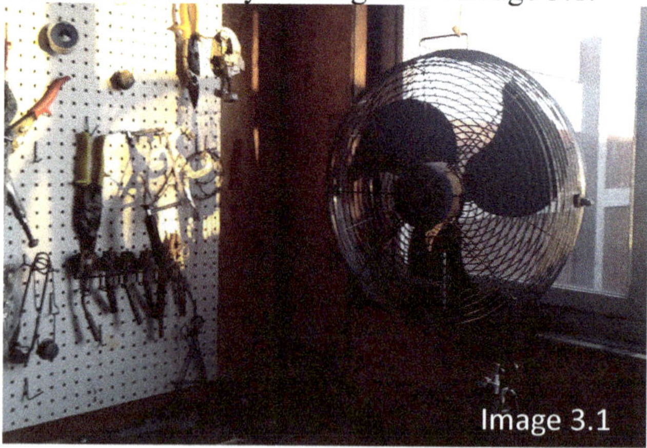

Image 3.1

It is tilted slightly toward my bench pulling the fumes directly away from me and my workspace.

I include a pegboard, Image 3.1, for organizing regularly used tools and an area for those that are in current use. Keep your workspace free of unnecessary objects. Your steel table and ceramic pads are the main occupants of the brazing area. I find it convenient to place goggles, a striker, pliers, and a quenching container filled with water nearby on an adjacent cement board work area.

Oxygen and acetylene tanks are nearby, lines kept out of the immediate range of torch flame and strapped to a wall or dolly such that there is little chance of them being knocked over. I also created a torch stand to hold the lighted torch when I change positions or quickly set up the next step in construction. Torch stands may be purchased, as well.

I set both gauges at three to five pounds of pressure (Image 3.2) when I use tips #4, #5, or #6 and three pounds (possibly less) when using #2 or #3 (instructions on pages 1 and 10). When not in use the tanks should be turned off and the torch lines purged: acetylene first, oxygen second. Then back off the gauge pressure until the spring is released. This is obvious when there is easy play in the handle of the gauge.

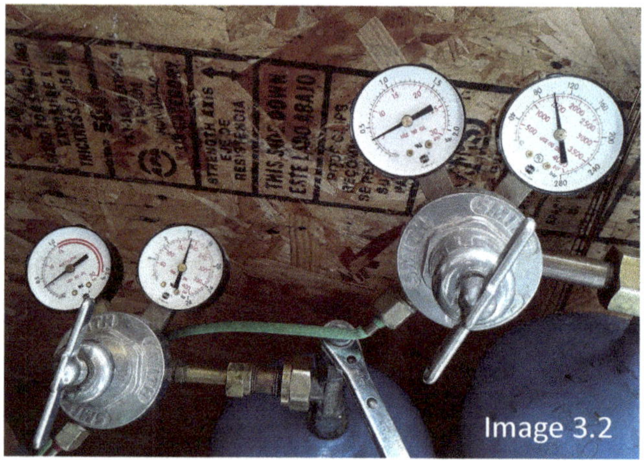

Image 3.2

I have a jewelry-style workbench for laying out small pieces and on which are trays to hold components for current projects. My flex shaft, angle grinder, cut off wheel tool, and a variety of attachments for these tools are quickly accessed from this bench as well.

You may include as many worktables and shelves as space allows and for what you feel is needed to organize projects, tools, and supplies.

CHAPTER 4

SAFETY

I am assuming that my audience is familiar with safety precautions prescribed for those working in the metal arts. Thus, I will focus on safety issues related to torch brazing. Central to this consideration is the proper setting up of both tanks and gauges by opening both tank valves as follows (making sure that torch valves are closed and the adjusting screws on both regulators are backed out). First, open acetylene valve 1/4 turn. Second, open oxygen valve full on. Next adjust both regulators to desired pressure settings and check each separately by opening and closing each torch valve and making sure they hold the desired pressure.

To light the torch, slightly open acetylene torch valve first and light with lighter or striker; adjust to where there is no smoke and gently open oxygen valve–adjust to neutral flame as described in Chapter 5. You are set to braze.

Extremely Important: *never* lubricate the brass fittings on your tanks!! They do not need it and to do so would lead to the possibility of an explosion.

BODY PROTECTION

Eyes - When brazing—goggles with at least #5 lens. When sanding, buffing, or neutralizing acid cleaning solutions—clear lenses, wraparound preferred. Face shield when wanted and needed.

Ears - Muffs or earplugs.

Skin - Gloves—blue nitrile and thin leather—a clear plastic face shield—yellow mustard (for burns).*

Lungs - Dust mask—exhaust fan. I avoid using toxic abrasives and cleaning solutions whenever possible (see Chapter 6 on cleaning finished artwork). Not only as protection for myself but also for the environment. The dilemma being where and how do we properly dispose of them?

Hair/Clothing - Hair tied back and/or hat and no loose clothing, i.e. ties or belts flying about, overly long or loose sleeves, anything that can easily catch fire or get snagged by a sander or rotary tool.

yellow mustard, conventional variety, sold at any grocery market is extremely useful to thwart the blistering of burns. It is necessary to stop what you are doing when you burn yourself, immediately apply the mustard (which I keep chilled in the fridge), and cover the area, being mindful that mustard stains. When I want to quickly return to my project, I squirt mustard into a nitrile glove, insert my injured hand/finger inside and return to work. Leave the mustard on for a few hours. I don't know why this works, but it does; better than any other remedy I have tried. Aloe vera is wonderfully soothing when applied after rinsing the area to remove the "magic mustard".

STUDIO

Exhaust Fan - With sufficient power to pull air out of studio and away from your face.

Fire extinguisher - (Or two).

Adequate electrical supply - Depending on tool requirements.

And as much organization as you can tolerate More is better. I dislike spending time looking for items that have migrated from their designated place. It is often a mystery to me as to who came into my studio and put an item where I can not find it. Especially since I live alone.

CHAPTER 5

**STEP – BY – STEP
BRAZING INSTRUCTIONS:
HOW TO CREATE
TWO PROJECT COMPONENTS
AND ONE FINISHED DESIGN
WITH TORCH BRAZING TECHNIQUES**

**PROJECT #1:
TEXTURE ON A CRESCENT MOON**

1. Set acetylene and oxygen torch pressures at 3 to 5 pounds. I am using a Smith Little Torch with a #4 tip. Image 3.2.

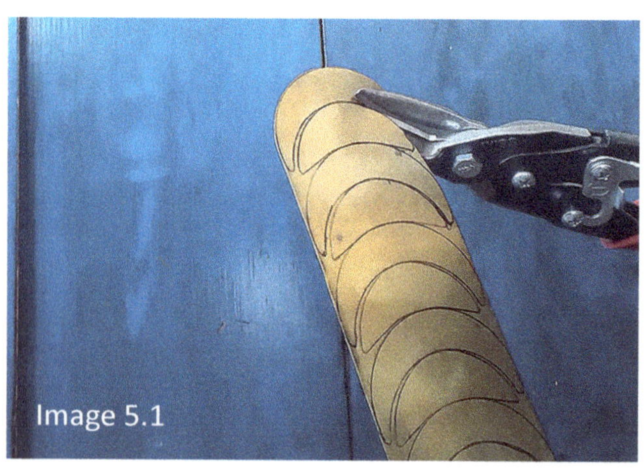

Image 5.1

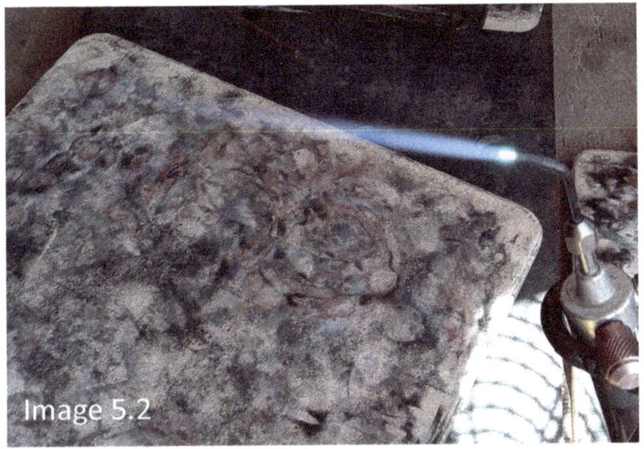

2. Collect project materials:
- In this case: cut, flattened, and sanded 22-gauge brass crescent moons to be textured. Again, note the angle of snips in relationship to metal. Image 5.1.
- Proper size bronze brazing rods: 1/16 X 36 and 3/32 X 36 inches. Samples: Image 2.1.
- Flux at the ready.

3. Turn on fan or other ventilation system.

4. Light torch with striker and adjust to neutral flame: where oxygen and acetylene meet to form a soft point. No feather (too much acetylene) or sharp blue flame (too much oxygen). Flame should be about 3/16 inch in length. Image 5.2.

Put on goggles.

5. Heat moon slightly and sprinkle with flux.

6. Preheat moon along with the end of a 3/32-inch bronze rod. You will need to periodically dip it into flux to assure flow of metal onto moon. I view this process as "texture painting with melting bronze"–creating pools, bumps, and craters (but no holes unless that is what you intend to make or just like the way they look). Leave the ends of the moon smooth, as they will be textured in the next steps. Image 5.3.

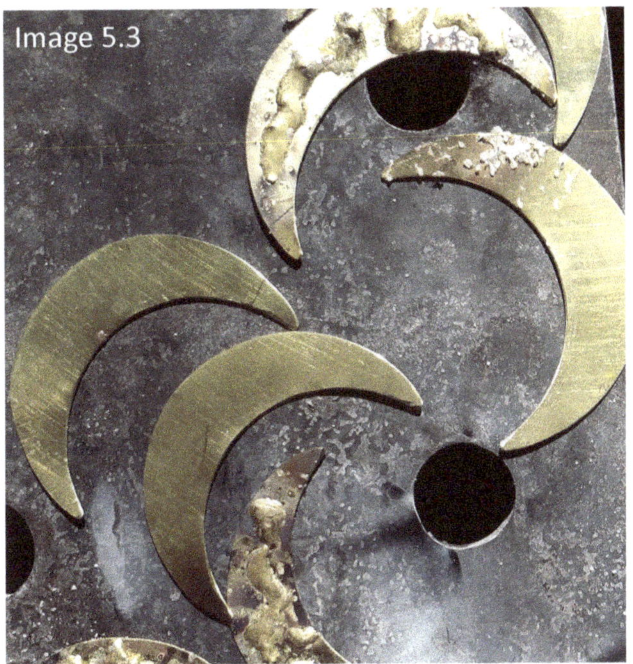

7. Turn down the torch and dip the heated 1/16-inch rod in flux.

8. Carefully heat and melt the rod onto each end of the moon. It is easy to burn these narrow areas and especially the ends (on any shape) during this process; so move your torch away from the moon when you see the metal getting too hot (visually very shiny and bright yellow). Then come back over the moon with the smaller rod, creating more textural detail to please your eye on the whole moon. Image 5.4.

9. This element is ready to be added to a project. Note: practicing on scrap metal is recommended before you attempt to texture a shape in which you have invested your valuable time and effort preparing.

This is a Bright Star and Buffalo design

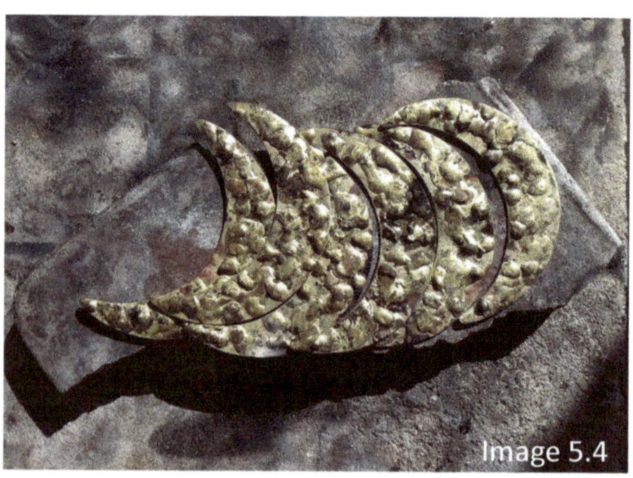
Image 5.4

PROJECT #2:
BRAZING TWO BRASS TRIANGLES
TO EACH OTHER

1. Set acetylene and oxygen torch pressures at 3 to 5 pounds. I am using a Smith Little Torch #4 tip. Image 3.2.

2. Collect project materials:
- In-house created—22-gauge brass triangles. I use two sizes in this design.

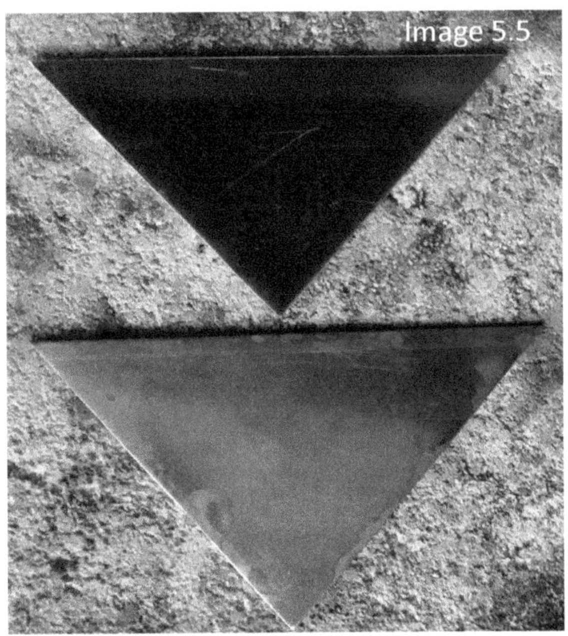

Larger is 1 ½ X 1 ½ inches and smaller is 1 ¼ X 1 ¼ inches. Image 5.5.
- 1/16-inch brazing rod.
- Flux at the ready.

3. Turn on fan or other ventilation system

4. Light torch with striker and adjust to neutral flame: where oxygen and acetylene meet to form a soft point. No feather (too much acetylene) or sharp blue flame (too much oxygen). Flame should be about 3/16-inch in length. Image 5.2. Put on goggles.

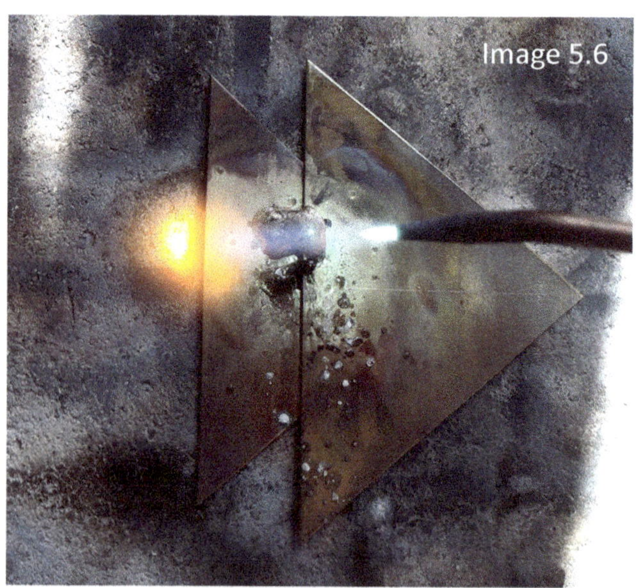

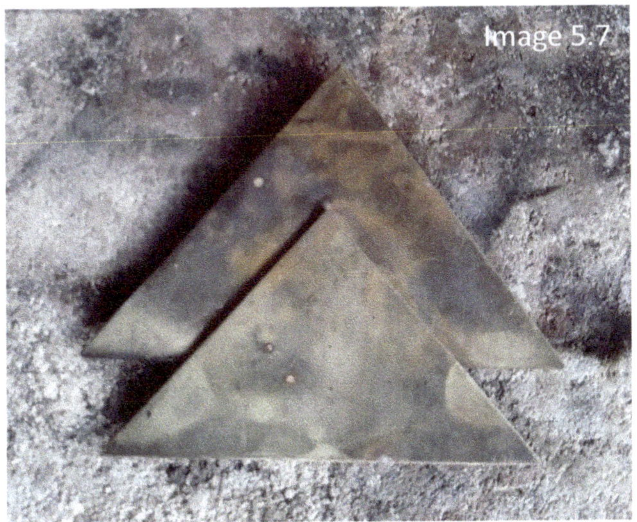

5. Align parts, preheat, and tack with brazing rod dipped in flux. Image 5.6.

6. The part is ready to be added to a project. Image 5.7. This is a Bright Star and Buffalo design.

PROJECT #3:
CREATE A WALL HOOK

1. Set acetylene and oxygen torch pressures at 3 to 5 pounds. I am using a Smith Little Torch with a #4 tip. Image 3.2.

2. Collect project materials:
- Brass keyhole bracket: manufactured by a local company using Bright Star and Buffalo design. Purchase at etsy: kjbsculpture. Image 5.8.
- Proper size bronze brazing rods: 1/16 X 36, 3/32 X 36, and 1/8 X 36 inches. Image 5.8.
- 1 inch 22-gauge brass disc. Image 5.8.
- Flux at the ready.

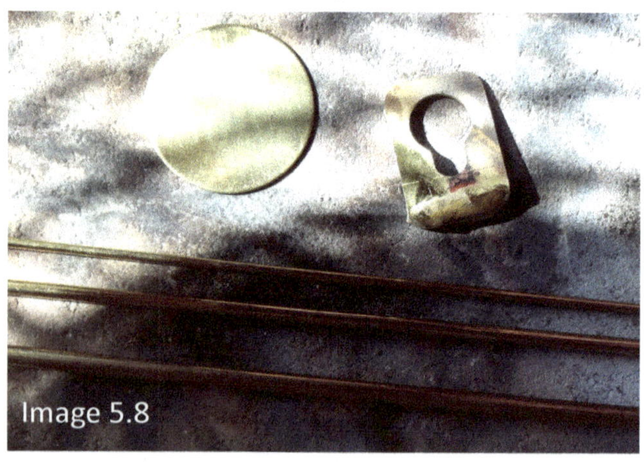

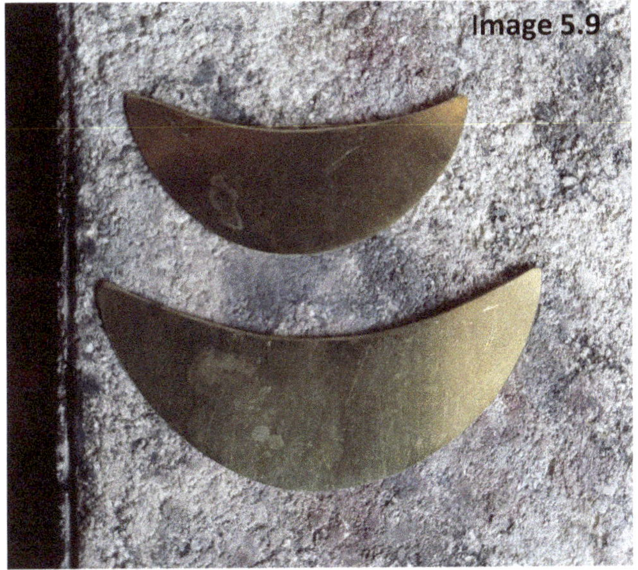

- Two in-house made—22-gauge brass crescent moons; cut, straightened, and sanded. Image 5.9. Each moon should be marked on its back at the center point for ease of placement.

3. Turn on fan or other ventilation system.

4. Light torch with striker and adjust to neutral flame: where oxygen and acetylene meet to form a soft point. No feather (too much acetylene) or sharp blue flame (too much oxygen). Flame should be about 3/16 in length. Image 5.2. Put on goggles.

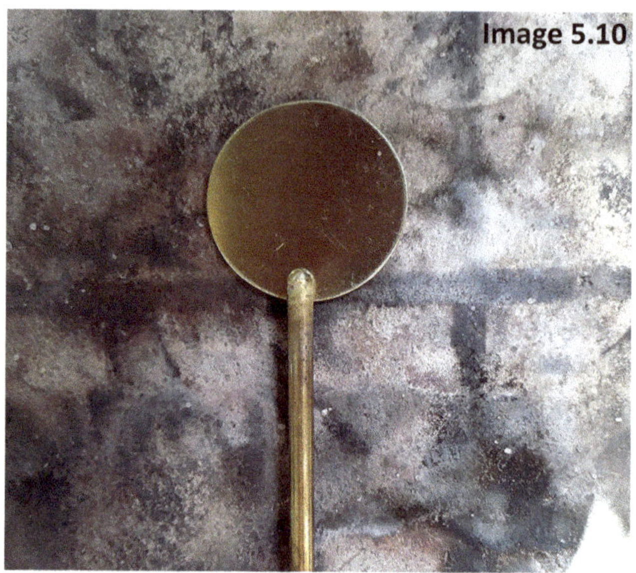

5. Place an 1/8-inch rod about 1/8 inch into the disc and align it with the center (of the disc). Preheat and braze in place using a 1/16-inch rod heated and dipped in flux. Check work to make sure alignment is true. Image 5.10.

6. Attach keyhole bracket in line with rod and at the very top of the disc with 1/16-inch rod. This is tricky. Keep your flame moving back and forth when metal is too hot (visually very shiny and bright yellow). Back off with your torch as well if necessary. It is easy to melt the disc or the bracket before it is attached.

The molten metal characteristically flows from the bracket to the disc. Image 5.11.

7. Align moons with unit created in steps five and six and braze to stem rod with an 1/16-inch rod. Visually check assembly to determine that alignment is true to design and adjust if necessary. Permanently attach. Image 5.12.

8. Clean in vinegar/salt/soap solution (recipe in Chapter 6) by soaking for 15 to 20 minutes, neutralizing, and rinsing in clear water.

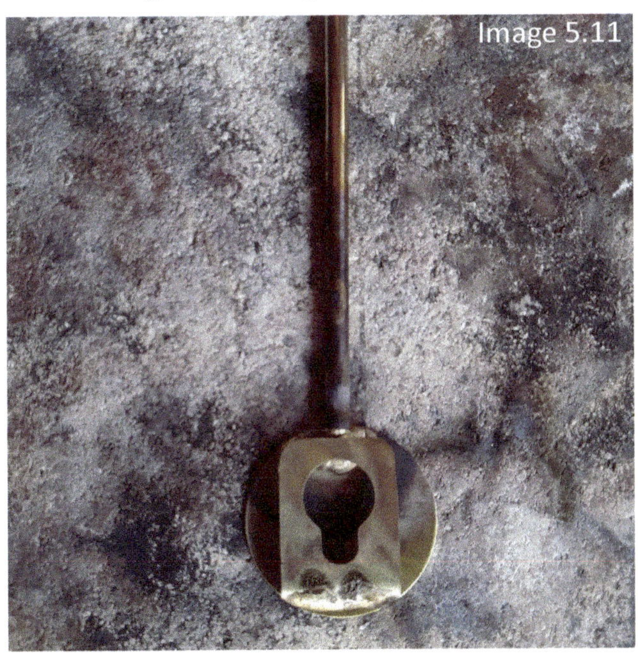

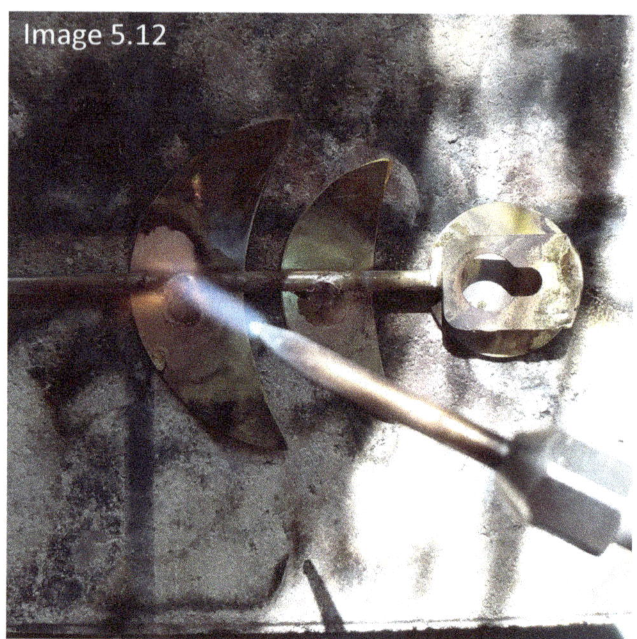

9. Form hook. Place stem rod in vise: Image 5.13. Begin heating the rod at desired length for finished hook. Create curved shape by continuing to heat the rod around loop, bending as you heat. The width of the hook is also up to you.

10. Complete hook. Align stem rod with center body of wall hook assembly. Image 5.13.

11. Cut hook at bottom edge of larger moon with cut-off tool. Clean up burrs on edge of cut. Image 5.14.

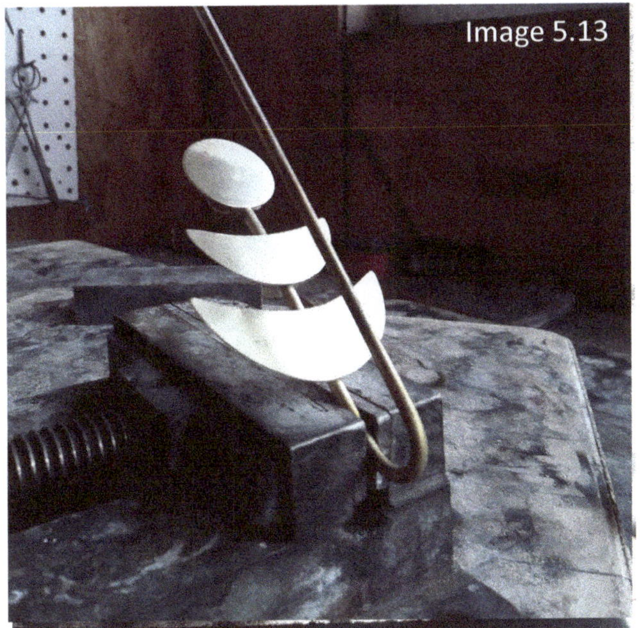

12. Finish as desired: polishing, brushing, patinating, etc.

Note: this hook is a Bright Star and Buffalo trademarked design: "M is for Moon" available for purchase in my etsy shop: kjbsculpture.

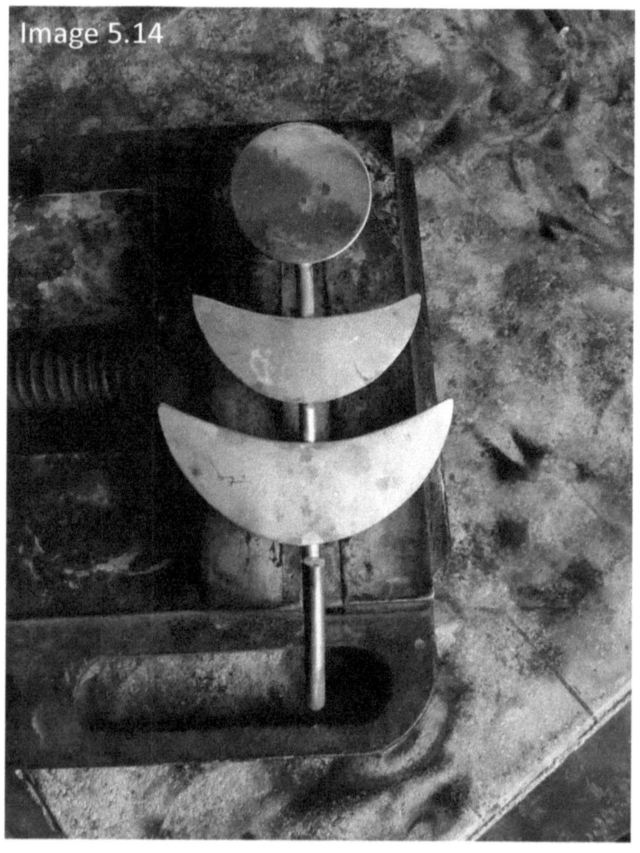

CHAPTER 6

CLEANING FINISHED ARTWORK

There are numerous traditional ways to clean finished work depending on the desired result. These include mechanical methods such as machine and hand sanding, wet and dry tumbling, chemical removal of tarnish and soldering residues, polishing with compounds, and using flexshaft or Dremel tools. There are many references to these methods readily available to the reader.

My view is less is more. What has become vitally important to me over time is not only my footprint on all levels but the impact of the use of toxic substances on my person and the environment. I researched ways to have the least impact and found that hunters who reload their brass shell casings use a combination of salt, vinegar, liquid soap, and water along with intermittent agitation or wet tumbling. Recipe:

- 1 quart warmish filtered or distilled water
- 1 cup white household vinegar
- 1 tablespoon salt
- 1 tablespoon liquid soap

Mix the ingredients and transfer to a hot pot, keeping the temperature low. Place finished pieces in this solution and carefully monitor the cleaning process, as copper flashing can quickly develop (or be uncovered?) on brass and bronze. These undesired oxides may be removed by putting the piece in a mixture consisting of 1/2 3% hydrogen peroxide and 1/2 warm pickle from your pickle pot for a minute or two and then rinsing, neutralizing and rinsing again. Copper is more forgiving.

The vinegar solution (perhaps this is where the term "pickle" originated?) may also be employed in a wet tumbler with good result. The solution is used at room temperature in this application. It takes 10 to 15 minutes in the tumbler with fresh solution; longer if it has degraded.

I also use Sparex (pickle) in recommended dilution, but rarely warm. I hold it in a hot pot for quick heat in case I want to use it that way; however, I find that the room temperature solution works well to clean bronze components by dunking artwork for two minutes or less.

For disposal, do not pour these acidic solutions down the sink! Thoroughly neutralize both by slowly adding baking soda until the solution stops fizzing when more baking soda is added. At that point, it should be a bright blue or turquoise color, is of acid pH and contaminated with copper (which is another reason for not disposing it down the drain). I let the water evaporate and save the powder to take to a hazardous waste collection site. A word of caution: *Do Not Breathe The Fumes* that are given off while neutralizing; proceed in a well-ventilated area and wear gloves and goggles.

At this juncture, it is up to the artist to decide how to finish a piece; polishing, buffing, wire brushing, or using steel wool as desired.

ARTIST'S NOTE

As you have likely noticed, I have not included brazing on copper in this manual. The reason for this is that the same techniques apply with the following adjustments: a slightly higher torch temperature is required. Despite this, there is less likelihood of burning through the shape on which you are brazing.

However it will be necessary to preheat the copper shape evenly to an orange color before beginning to texture it. Otherwise, the same steps as illustrated in Chapter 5, Project #1 may be followed with good result. Attaching two copper forms to each other is virtually the same as that of attaching two brass ones with the exception of the need for higher heat: reference Chapter 5, Project #2. Copper becomes softer than brass and may need to be work hardened after heating, using traditional techniques.

ABOUT THE AUTHOR

I grew up getting my hands dirty in the soft mud of my Colorado farm home on the Arkansas River. My first encounter with welding was with my father, William. We made wildly primitive electric "farmer" welds on infrastructure and equipment. My earliest desire was to become a "lawyer for the people" yet after attending the University of Colorado for a year, I determined that this was an inappropriate fit.

For the next few years I explored various art forms such as drawing, sculpture, theater, and music. It wasn't until I picked up my guitar, migrated to New Orleans, Louisiana in the early 1970s singing and playing music on its famous streets, however, that I connected with metal sculpting. Here, I fell in love with John Potts, and the work he did with his hands: oxygen-acetylene torch brazing with bronze brazing rods. He upcycled copper tubing, non-ferrous wire, sheet copper, and sheet brass, scavenged from local junk yards. These materials metamorphosed into fountains, steamboats, and landscape pieces of metal art under his expert hands. John had carved out a niche in the New Orleans art scene and became my husband and first mentor.

I soon discovered that torch brazing is immensely different from electric welding, and has limited but very specific industrial uses.

When employed for connecting metal in an artistic sense, there are not a lot of rules. Technique is developed through mentoring, education, trial and error, and perseverance. Included, obviously, must be desire and a commitment to develping skill over time. I have designed workshops that promise to showcase the techniques described in this manual, in an effort to shorten the learning curve for acolytes.

I am careful to make pieces that have intrinsic value for prospective clients being mindful that Mother Earth has gifted us with many of the substances I and any metal craft person uses. I am also committed to designs (my own and collaborations) that incorporate my scraps for direct recycling purposes.
Creating art is a gift; for you and the world so now go make it with your own hands, please!

P.S. Why the mysterious art of brazing? No matter how many pieces I make or how long I work with these materials and techniques, they continually reveal themselves to me. All I need to bring are my hands full of wonder.

YOUR NOTES

34